Notes on the 5th String.

Here you will find the notes on the **5th string**. Because the notes go below the musical stave we need extra lines. These are called **Ledger Lines**. Study through the exercises then have a go at Drunken Sailor on page 4. For this song we use only the **C** but gives you more chance to practise 1/8th beats and reading some ledger line notes.

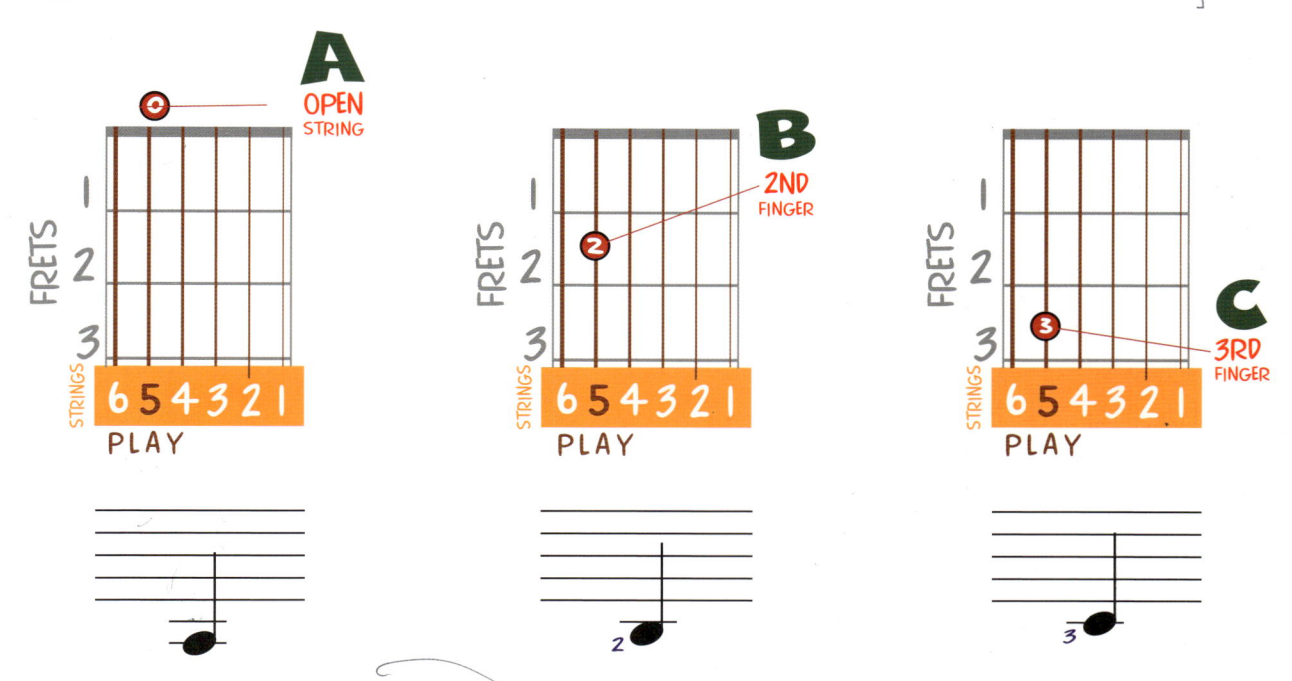

A — OPEN STRING

B — 2ND FINGER

C — 3RD FINGER

W is a **whole note** it's worth **4 beats**

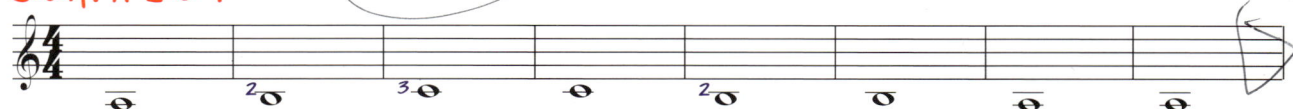

count: A 2 3 4

H is a **Half note** it's worth **2 beats**

count: A 2 A 2

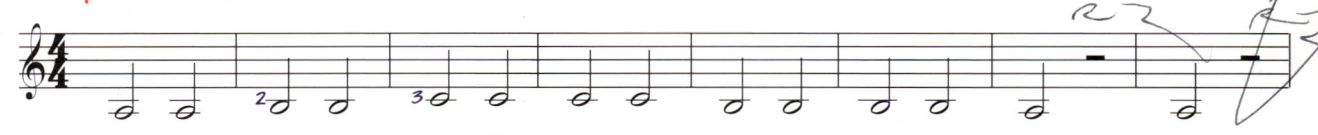

Q is a **Quarter note** only worth **1 beat**

count: A A A A

Session 21

FIFTH STRING

Session 21

What shall we do with the drunken sailor?

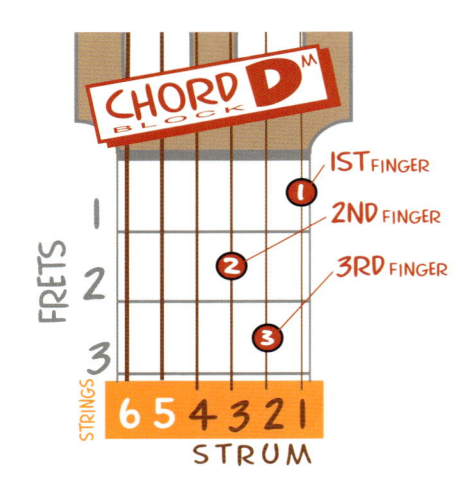

CHORD Dm BLOCK
- 1st Finger
- 2nd Finger
- 3rd Finger
Strings: 6 5 4 3 2 1 — STRUM

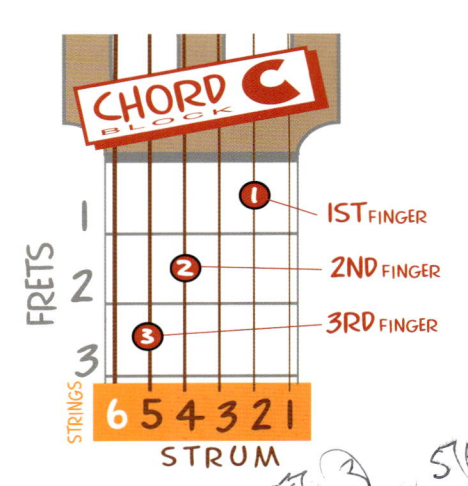

CHORD C BLOCK
- 1st Finger
- 2nd Finger
- 3rd Finger
Strings: 6 5 4 3 2 1 — STRUM

| Dm | / | / | / | Dm | / | / | / |

What shall we do with the drunken sailor,

| C | / | / | / | C | / | / | / |

What shall we do with the drunken sailor,

| Dm | / | / | / | Dm | / | / | / |

What shall we do with the drunken sailor,

| C | / | / | / | Dm | / | / | / |

Early in the morning?

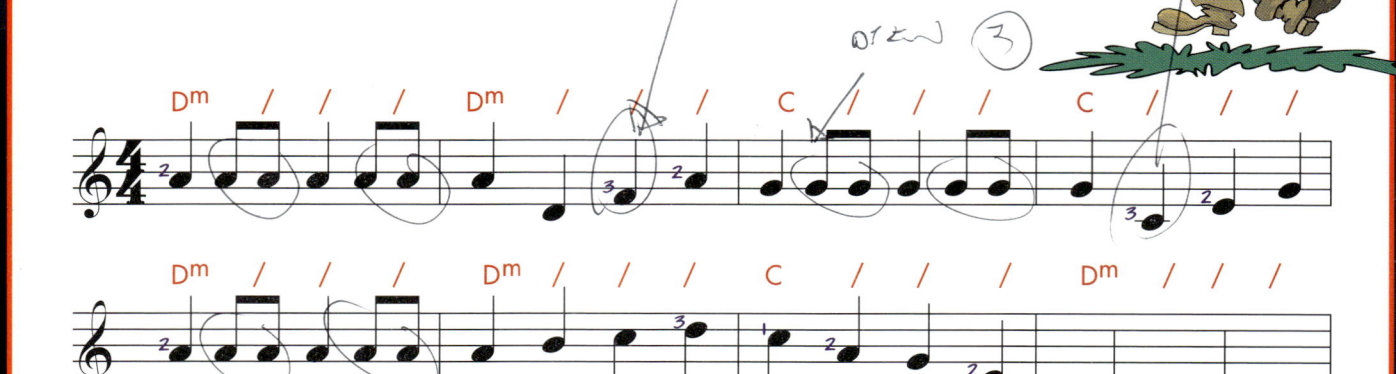

©2005 by Southern Counties Music Publishing. Photocopying is illegal.

FIFTH STRING

Session 21

Heave Ho!

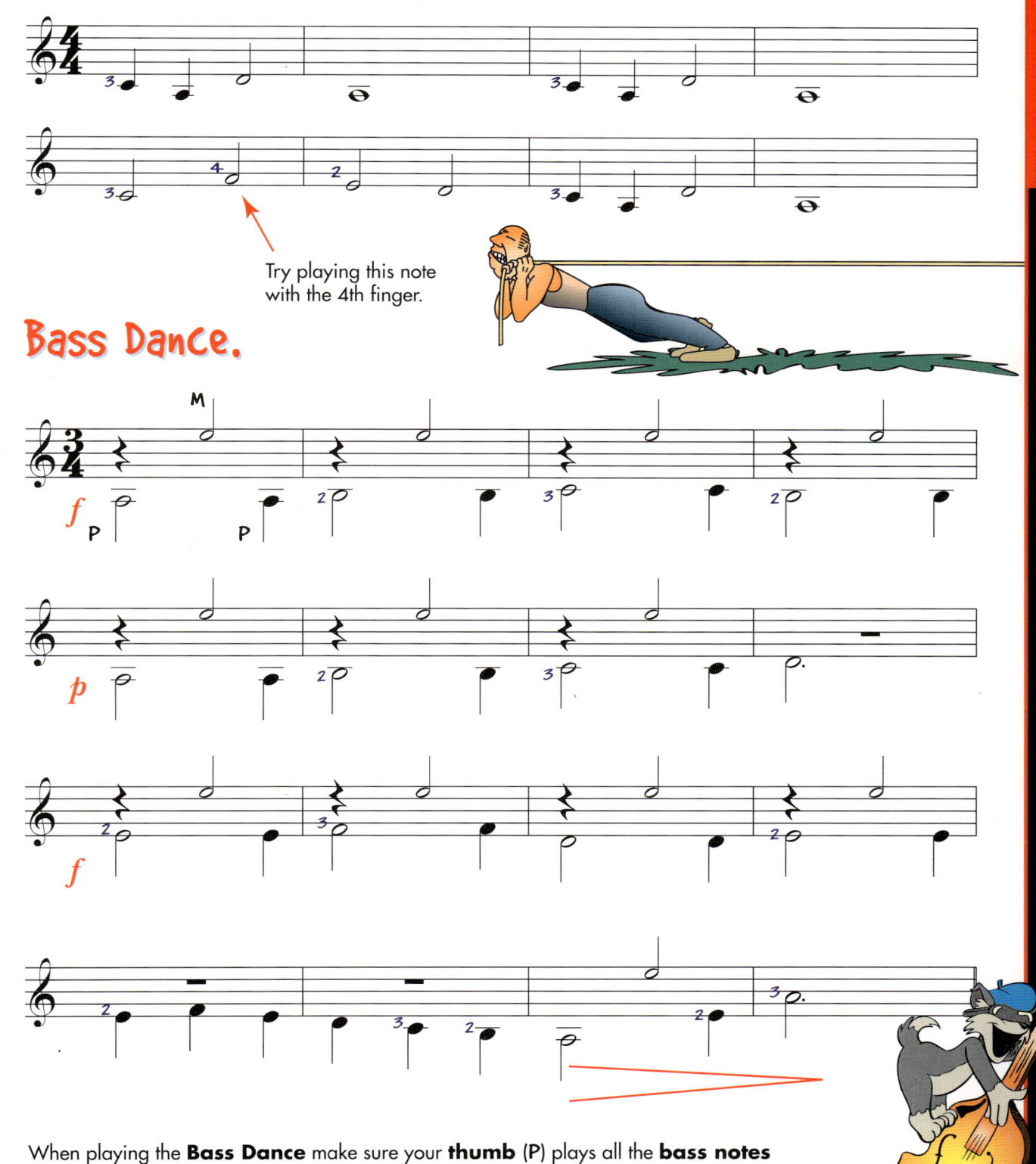

Try playing this note with the 4th finger.

Bass Dance.

When playing the **Bass Dance** make sure your **thumb (P)** plays all the **bass notes** and your **middle finger (M)** plays the **open E** string.

©2005 by Southern Counties Music Publishing. Photocopying is illegal.

FIFTH STRING

Session 21

Scale of C major.

Here you will find the **C Major Scale**.
There are many different kinds of scales but **C Major Scale** is known as the **Natural Scale**.

Time yourself playing it forwards.

Time week 1: ☐ secs   Time week 2: ☐ secs

Time yourself playing it backwards.

Time week 1: ☐ secs   Time week 2: ☐ secs

Time yourself playing it forwards and backwards.

Time week 1: ☐ secs   Time week 2: ☐ secs

This piece is called 5-1.

It covers all notes from the **5th string** to the **1st**.

©2005 by Southern Counties Music Publishing. Photocopying is illegal.

SIXTH STRING

Notes on the 6th String.

Here you will find the notes on the **6th string**. You may notice how the finger numbers and fret numbers are exactly the same as the **first string.** This is because the first string is also called **E** and will mirror the same sound but at a higher pitch.
Have a go at **high E** and **low E** and hear the difference.

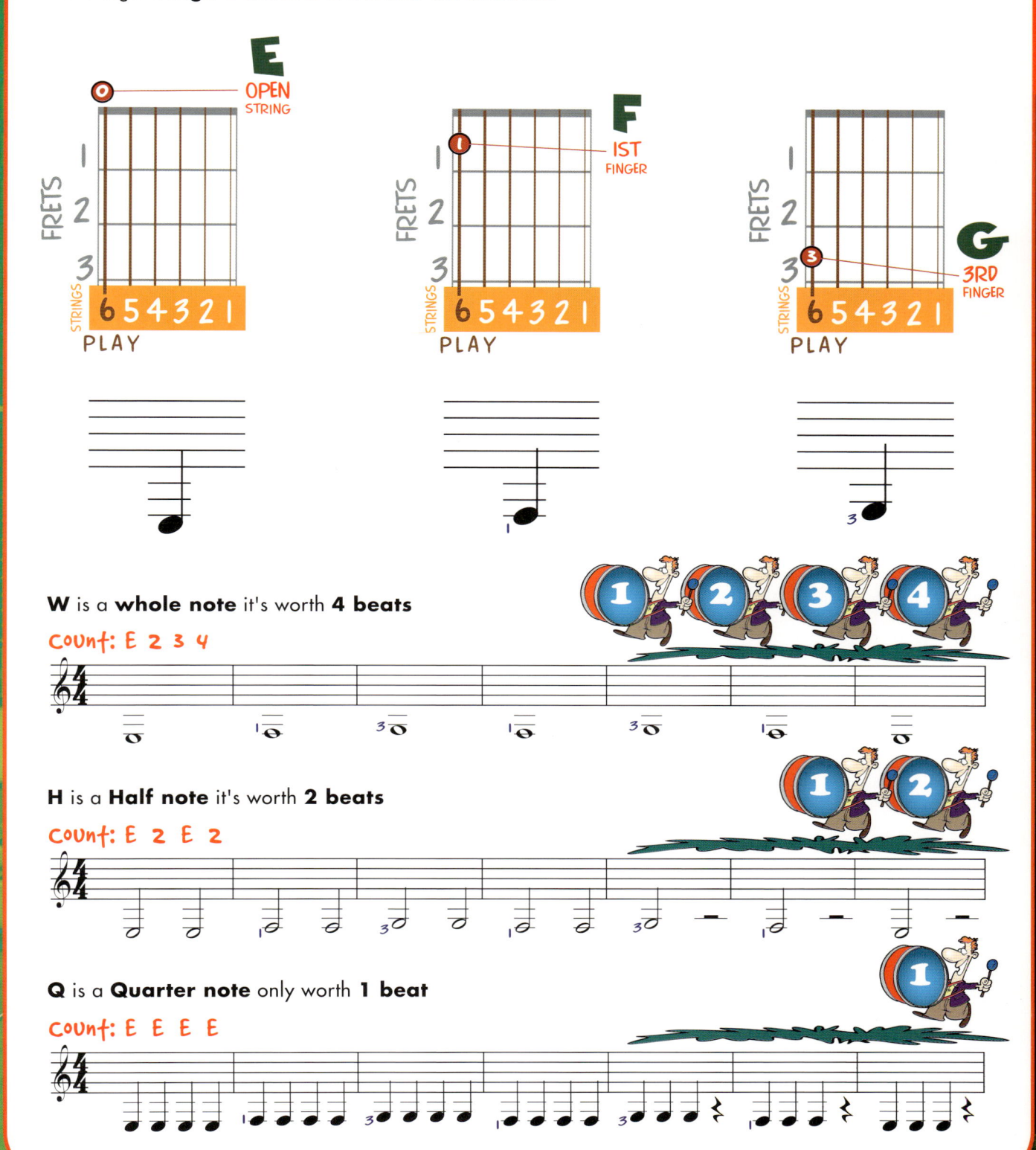

Session 22

E OPEN STRING

F 1ST FINGER

G 3RD FINGER

W is a **whole note** it's worth **4 beats**

count: E 2 3 4

H is a **Half note** it's worth **2 beats**

count: E 2 E 2

Q is a **Quarter note** only worth **1 beat**

count: E E E E

©2005 by Southern Counties Music Publishing. Photocopying is illegal.

Session 22

Little brother, big brother.

Sight Read.

Fastest gun in the west.

Here we have a **new game** called **"Fastest gun in the West"**. Starting on the **open 6th string** play all the notes in the first position up to the first string. You should try to play all these notes in **under 5 seconds**. If you go under 5 seconds you will be the fastest gun in the west.

Time week 1: _____ secs   **Time week 2:** _____ secs

©2005 by Southern Counties Music Publishing. Photocopying is illegal.

Three New Chords...

Here you will find 3 new chords: **A, D & E7.**

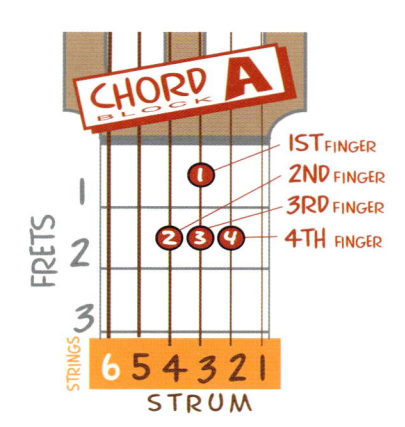

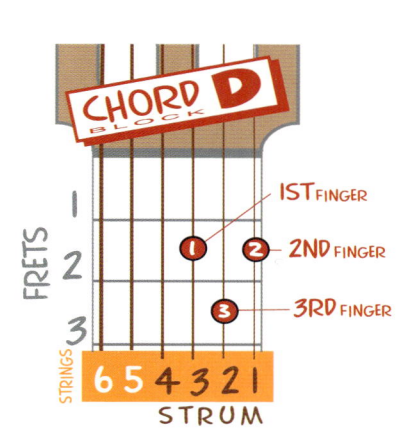

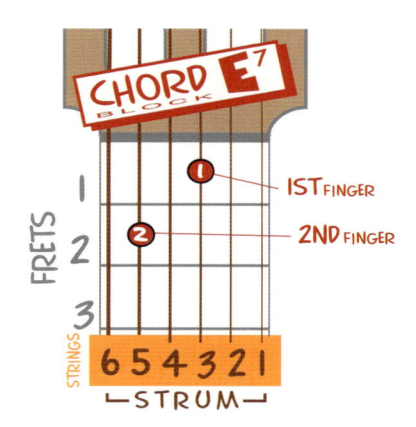

CHORD A
- 1ST FINGER
- 2ND FINGER
- 3RD FINGER
- 4TH FINGER

FRETS 1, 2, 3
STRINGS 6 5 4 3 2 1
STRUM

CHORD D
- 1ST FINGER
- 2ND FINGER
- 3RD FINGER

FRETS 1, 2, 3
STRINGS 6 5 4 3 2 1
STRUM

CHORD E7
- 1ST FINGER
- 2ND FINGER

FRETS 1, 2, 3
STRINGS 6 5 4 3 2 1
STRUM

The reason we play the **A chord** with fingers 2, 3 & 4 is so the finger behind can slide up and down for the D Triangle and **E7 chord.**

Remember the **first finger** never comes off the **3rd string** for this sequence.

Boogie Woogie.

This is a new sign: `·/.` and this means repeat the previous bar.

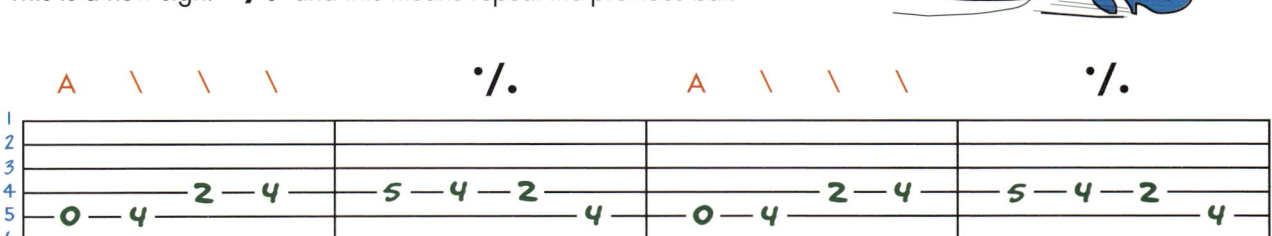

```
A \ \ \           ·/.        A \ \ \           ·/.
                2—4    5—4—2                  2—4    5—4—2
    0—4                    4      0—4                    4


D \ \ \           ·/.        A \ \ \           ·/.
    0—4         2—4    5—4—2                  2—4    5—4—2
                           4      0—4                    4


E7 \ \ \          D \ \ \         A \ \ \          A
              0                      0—2                2
        1—2                 0—4              2—4       
    2                                   0—4         0
```

Session 22

Session 23

The Tie.

The **Tie** is a **curved line** between **two notes** of the **same pitch**. The **first note is played** and the **second note is held** for however long the note is written. The first example is with open strings.

Count: E 2 3 Hold 2 3

Notice how, when the note has an **up stem**, the **tie** is written **below the notes**. When the note has a **down stem**, it is **written above**.

Comin' round the mountain...

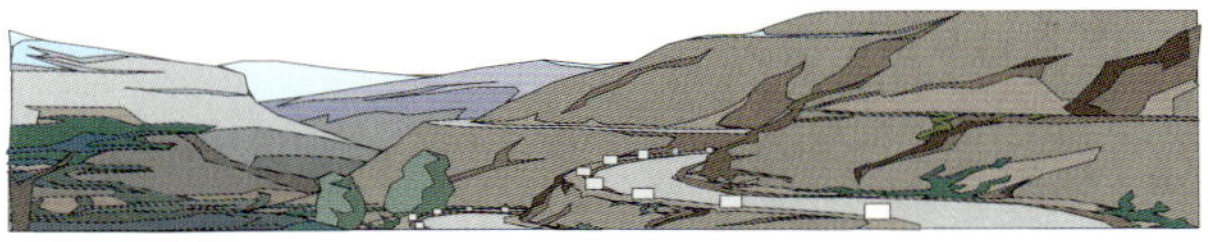

Here you will find some **new chords**.

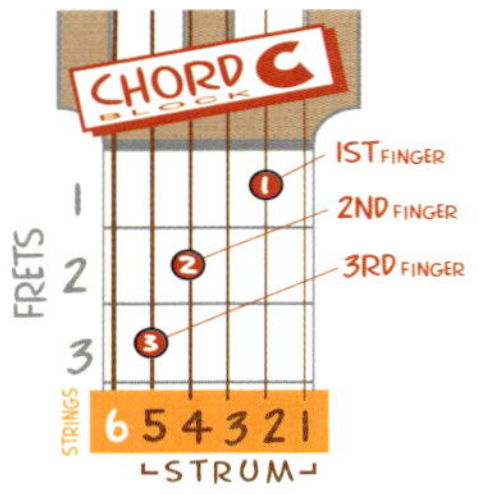

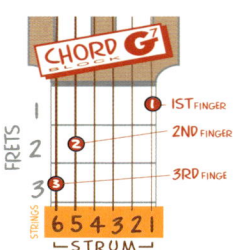

Start playing here

```
C        /        /        /        /        /
```
She'll be comin' round the mountain when she comes,
```
/        C        /        /        /        G7       /        /
```
She'll be comin' round the mountain when she comes,
```
/        C        /        /        /
```
She'll be comin' round the mountain,
```
F        /        /        /
```
Comin' round the mountain,
```
C        /        G7       /        C        /        /
```
Comin' round the mountain when she comes.

©2005 by Southern Counties Music Publishing. Photocopying is illegal.

Double workout.

This is a two part exercise.

Part 1

Don't worry to much, all this involves is **reading** and **playing** two notes at the **same time**.

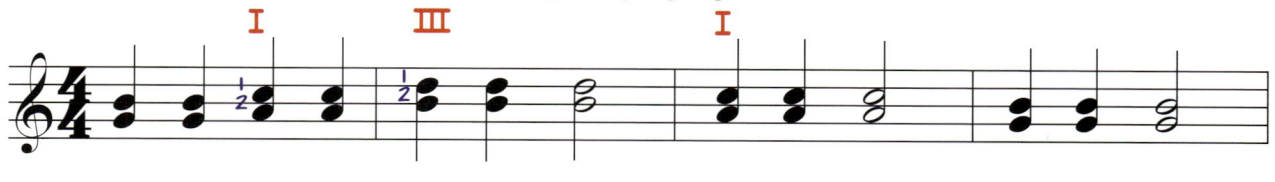

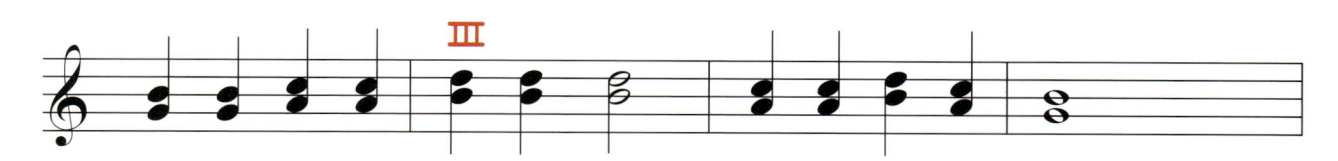

In **bar two** you may notice **III** written above. This means **3rd position.** If you take your **1st** and **2nd** finger on the **left hand** and **slide** them up to the **3rd** and **4th fret** you will be able to find **D** & **G**.

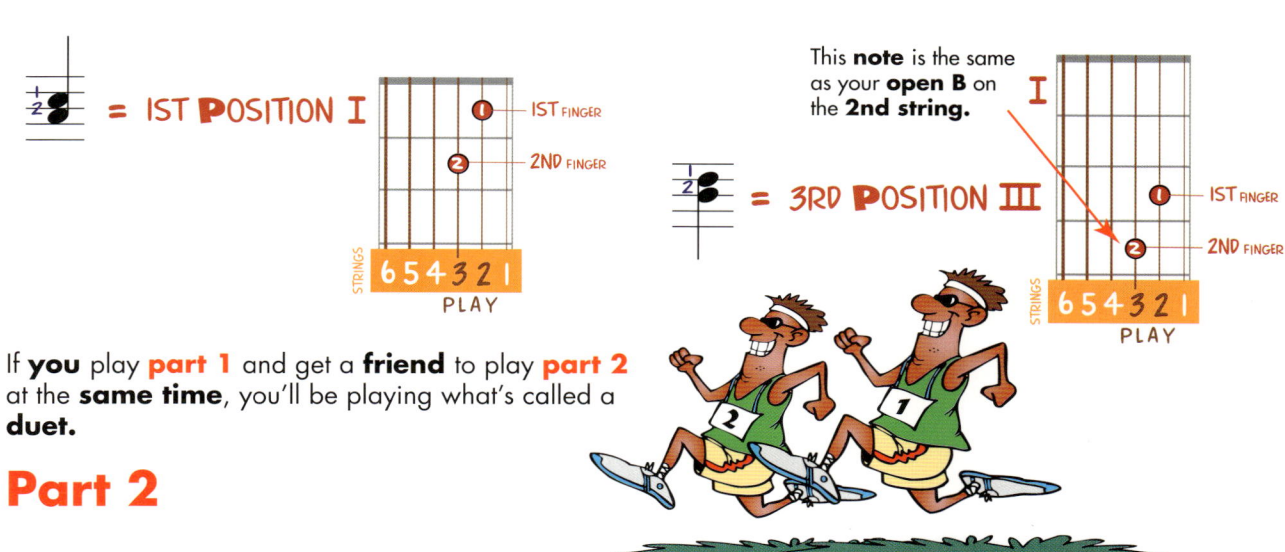

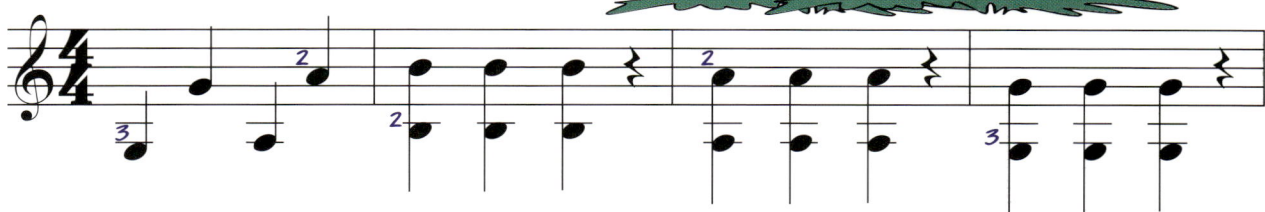

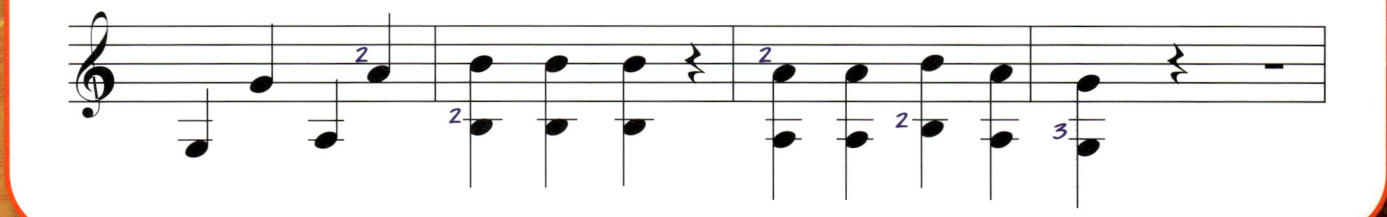

= IST POSITION I

= 3RD POSITION III

This **note** is the same as your **open B** on the **2nd string.**

If **you** play **part 1** and get a **friend** to play **part 2** at the **same time**, you'll be playing what's called a **duet.**

Part 2

©2005 by Southern Counties Music Publishing. Photocopying is illegal.

Session 25

Sharps #.

Here you will find a new musical symbol called a **sharp**. A sharp increases a note by **one semitone** or on the guitar **one fret.**

SHARP EXERCISE.

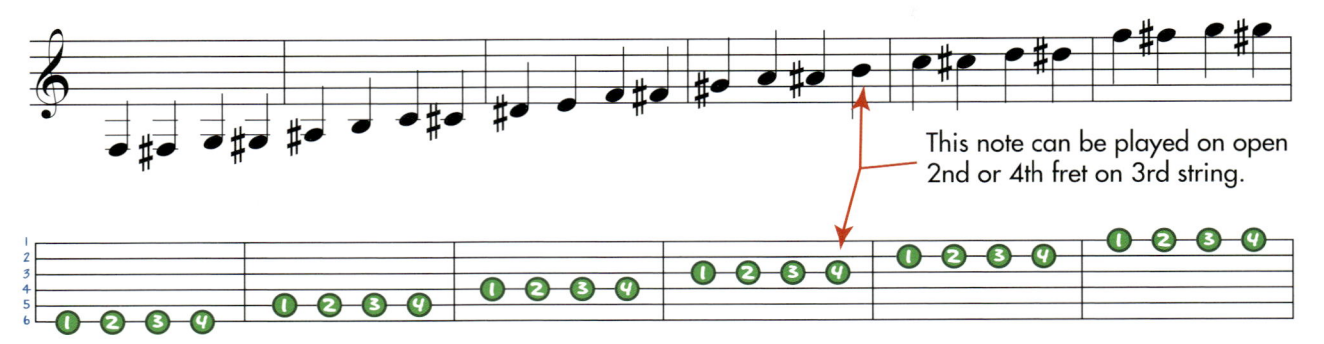

This note can be played on open 2nd or 4th fret on 3rd string.

For this exercise we have used tab to accompany the music and help you find the notes.

Scale of G using F#.

The scale of **G major** has **one sharp**. The sharp is **F#**. Notice how the middle of the box is on the **F line.**

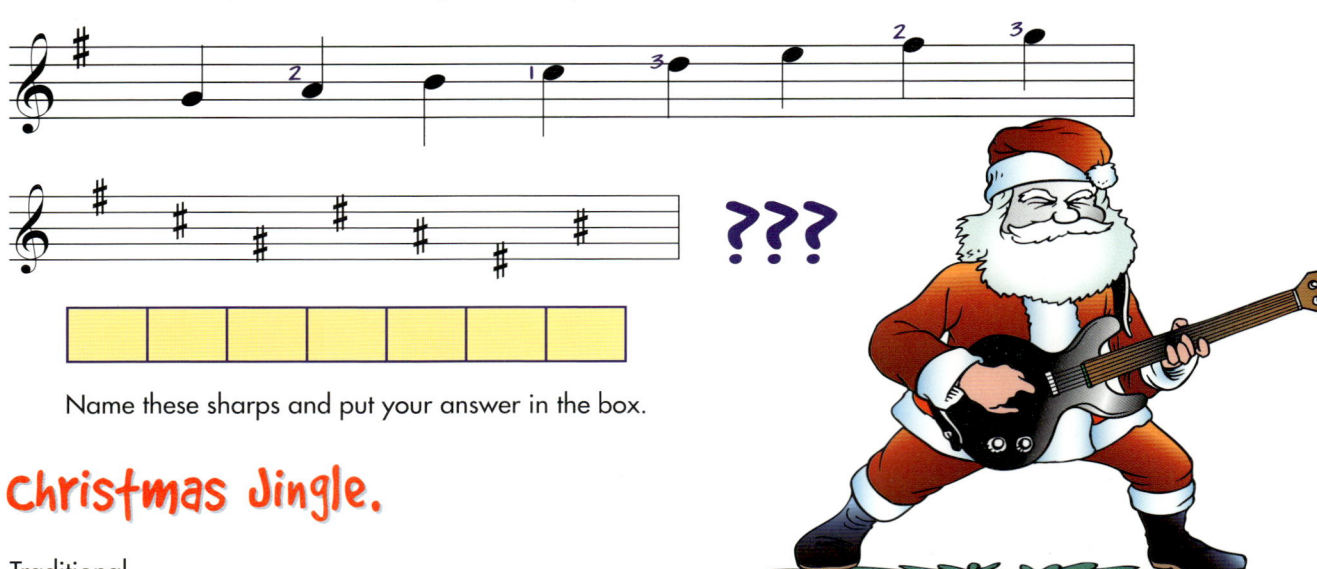

???

Name these sharps and put your answer in the box.

Christmas Jingle.

Traditional.

Here you will find a Christmas jingle in the key of **G major**. Don't forget to **play** all the F's as **F sharp**.

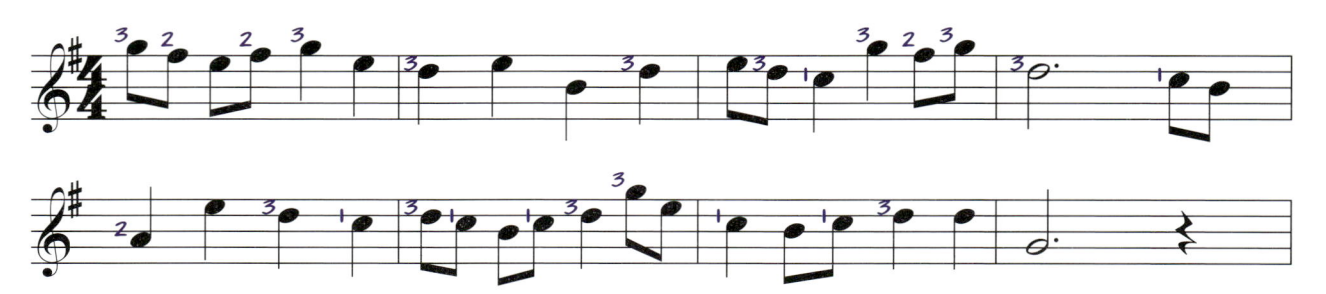

©2005 by Southern Counties Music Publishing. Photocopying is illegal.

Inspector.

This piece is in the **key** of **A^M**.
The key of **A^M** has no **Sharps** or **Flats** in the **signature**. Here we have to use an **accidental** (which means you add the sharp sign (♯) **next** to the note, for that bar only.

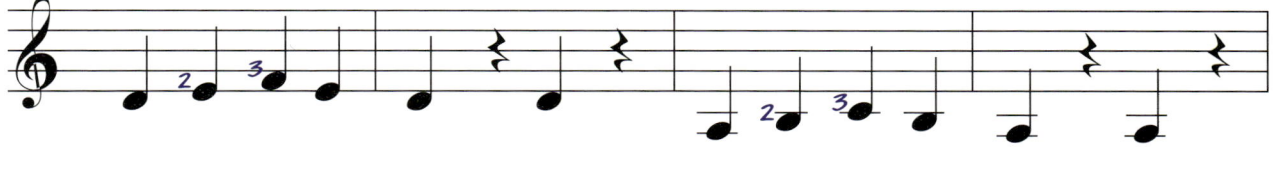

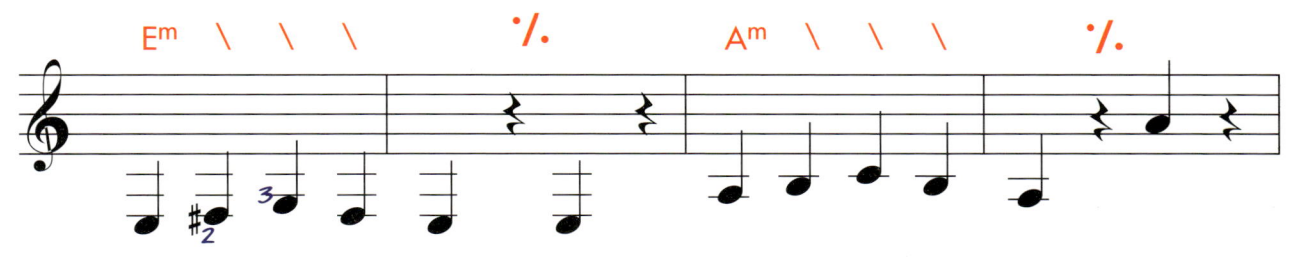

Here we have **three new chords** for this great piece called **'Inspector'**.
You can retrain your knowledge of **Bass Notes** and learn two new chords **A^M** and **E^M**.
You should remember the **D^M** from the song 'Drunken Sailor'.

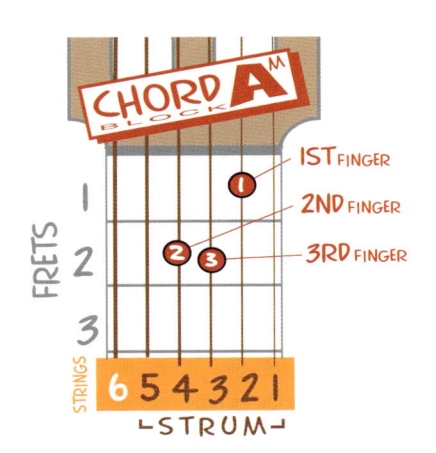

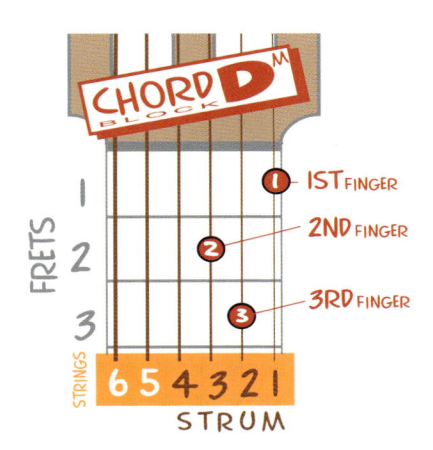

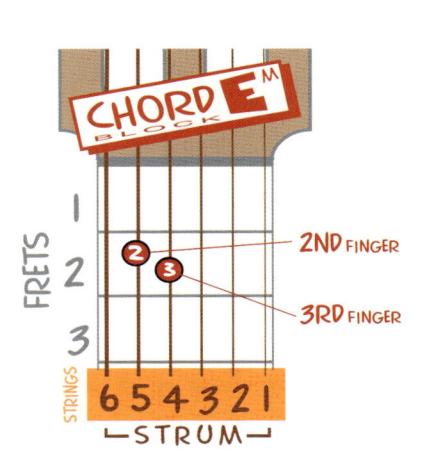

Session 26

Flats ♭.

We will now cover another new musical symbol called the **flat**. The flat **lowers a note** by **one semitone** or **one fret** on the guitar.

FLAT EXERCISE.

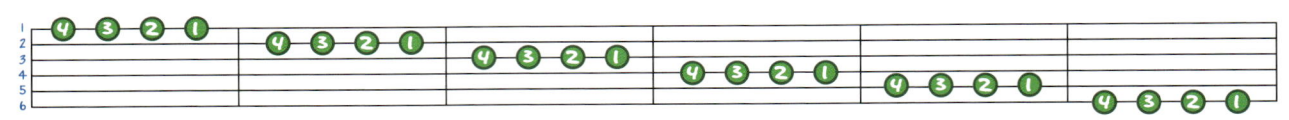

For this exercise we have used **tab** to accompany the music and help you find the notes.

Scale of F major using B♭.

The scale of **F major** has **one flat**. The flat is **B♭**. Notice how the **symbol** is **placed** on the **B line**.

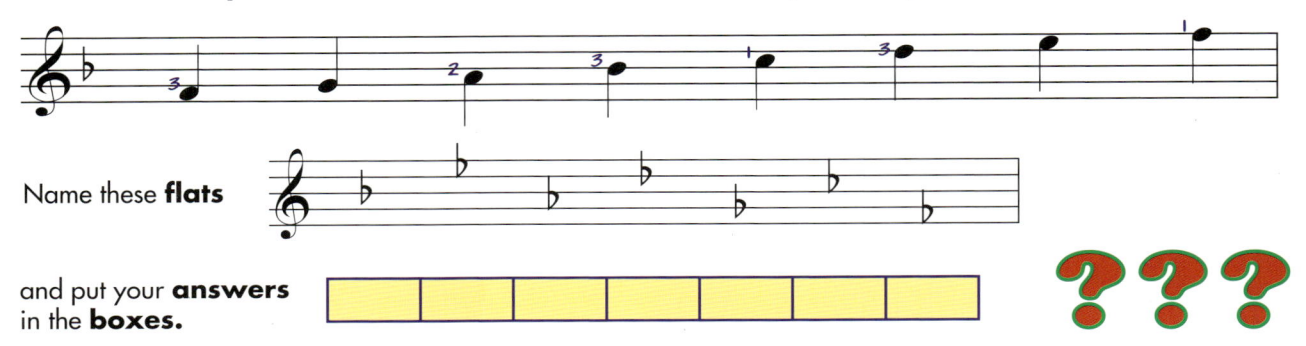

Name these **flats** and put your **answers** in the **boxes**.

Time yourself playing it forwards.
Time week 1: ___ secs   **Time week 2:** ___ secs

Time yourself playing it backwards.
Time week 1: ___ secs   **Time week 2:** ___ secs

Time yourself playing it forwards and backwards.
Time week 1: ___ secs   **Time week 2:** ___ secs

LOOKING AT KEY SIGNATURE

Frère Jacques is in the **key of F**. Because it uses the same notes from the **scale of F** it holds the same **signature**. A **B♭** is placed before the **time signature** and this means you must **flatten every B** you see in the music.

In case you can't find the **B♭** we have put it into a **chord block** for you to see.

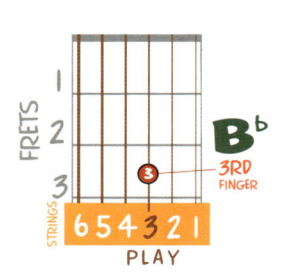

B♭ — 3RD FINGER

©2005 by Southern Counties Music Publishing. Photocopying is illegal.

Frère Jacques. Traditional French.

This is another two part exercise.

Part 1

LOOKING AT KEY SIGNATURE

Frère Jacques is in the **key of F**. Because it uses the same notes from the **scale of F** it holds the same **signature**. A **B♭** is placed before the **time signature** and this means you must **flatten every B** you see in the music.

In case you can't find the **B♭** we have put it into a **chord block** for you to see.

Below is a **Bass Line** that has been arranged to accompany the top line. Get your **Training Partner** to play **Part 1** whilst you play **Part 2** and vice versa.

Part 2

©2005 by Southern Counties Music Publishing. Photocopying is illegal.

Session 27

The Natural ♮.

This is the last of the symbols we will look at in this book. This symbol will **restore** a **note** to its **original pitch**. Try the example below.

Natural in the **Trebles** exercise.

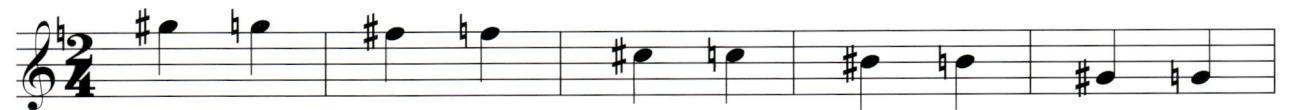

Natural in the **Basses.**

Naturally good!

I to II to III = slide from **1st** to **2nd** to **3rd** position.

©2005 by Southern Counties Music Publishing. Photocopying is illegal.

Dotted note fun.

In this workout we will look at **dotted quarter notes** (or **dotted crotchets**).
The **dot** after the note means add **half as much again** to the **length** of the note it's after.

EXAMPLES:

𝅝. = 4 + 2 = 6 beats

𝅗𝅥. = 2 + 1 = 3 beats

♩. = 1 + ½ = 1½ beats

The **trickier** notes to count are the **1 beat notes**
To break down this **rhythm** follow the chart below.

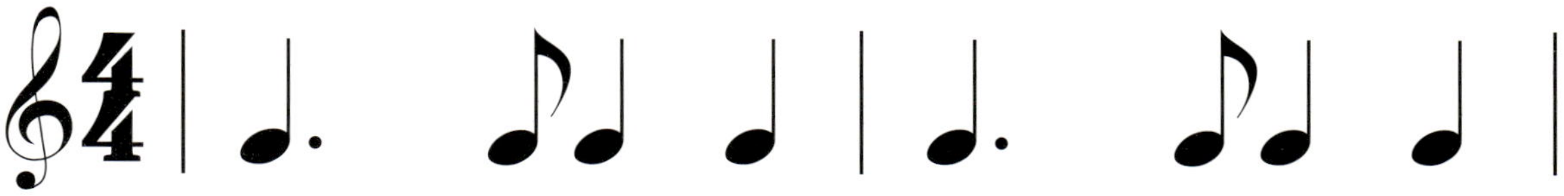

| 1 + 2 + 3   4 | 1 + 2 + 3   4 |

or think of... | Bob   the Buil - der | Bob   the Buil - der |

CLAPPING RHYTHMS

Workout 1

Workout 2

Workout 2

Session 28

construct it!

Session 28

Here we take the **dotted rhythm** and **build** into it our new piece called **"Construct it!"**

If you use your **4th finger** on the 'd' here...

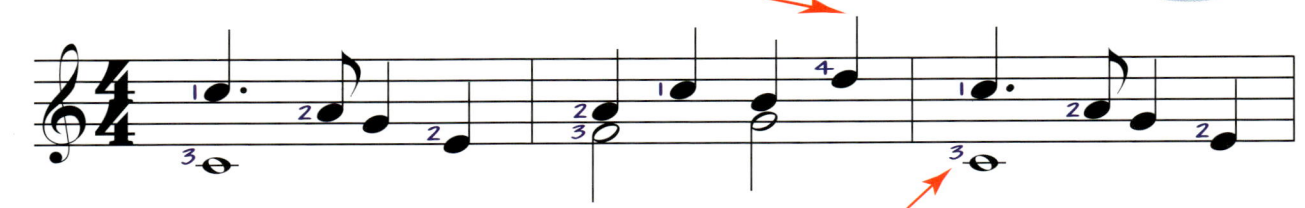

your **3rd finger** will be quicker getting to the 'c' with the **bass** here.

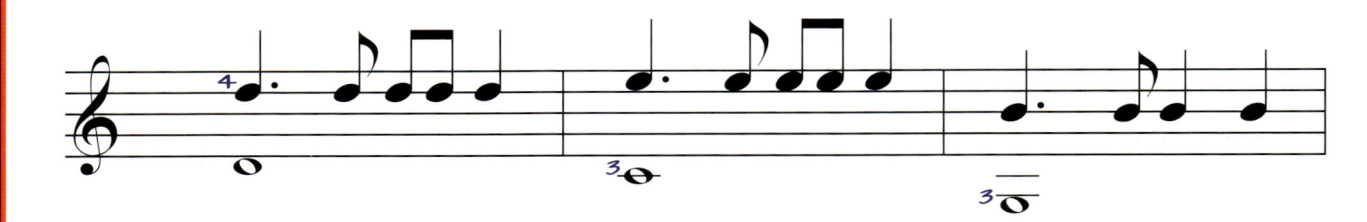

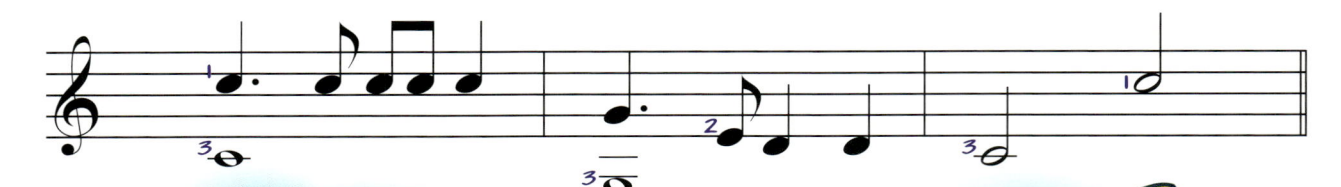

©2005 by Southern Counties Music Publishing. Photocopying is illegal.

Scarborough Fair.

Are you going to Scarborough fair?
Parsley, sage, rosemary and thyme.

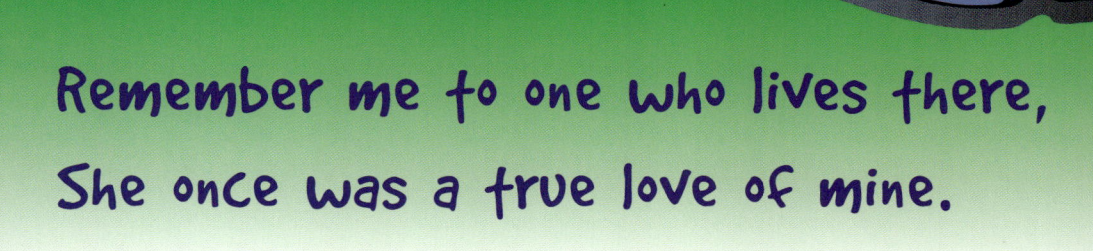

Remember me to one who lives there,
She once was a true love of mine.

Session 29

Triple note right hand game.

On this **game** we will pull **3 strings** at the same time.   **P I M A** = 4 3 2 1 (string numbers).

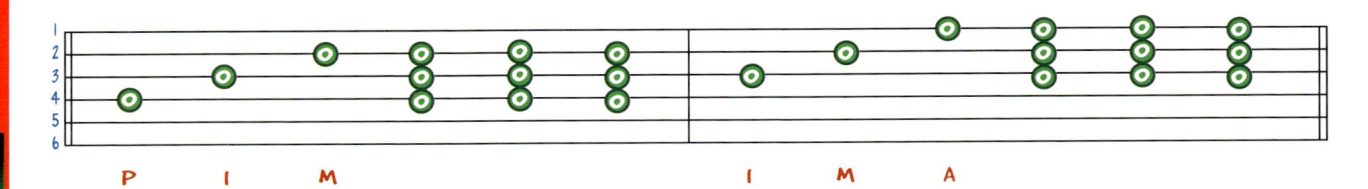

                P   I   M   I   M   A

On **bar 1** your start with **P I M**, then you **pull all 3** with **P I M**.

Then on **bar 2** you start **I M A** and **pull all 3** with **I M A**.

Don't forget to **repeat** the **sequence** and **time yourselves**.

Time week 1: _____ secs

Time week 2: _____ secs

Triple the fun.

Here you will find a similar session to before, except you see **3 notes at once**. For this exercise **pulgar P** should **play string number 4** and **I** & **M** play **3** & **2**.

P I M

STRINGS 6 5 **4 3 2** 1
PLAY

Easy as ABC. (first string)

Session 30

5th fret   7th fret   8th fret

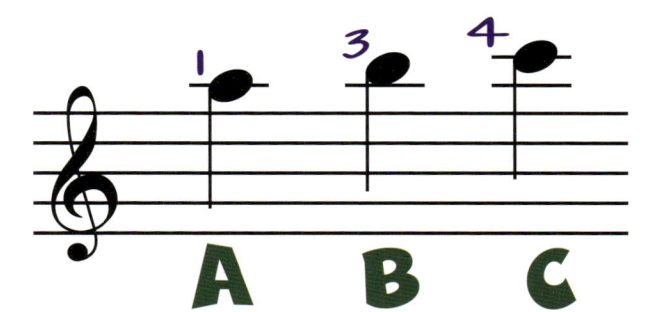

A   B   C

We will now look at notes **above 'A for Aeroplane'**. The two further notes for this exercise are **B** and **C**.

TIP: If you stay in the **5th position** you will use one finger per note.
LEFT HAND: 1st Finger = **A**, 3rd Finger = **B**, 4th Finger = **C**.

5TH POSITION V

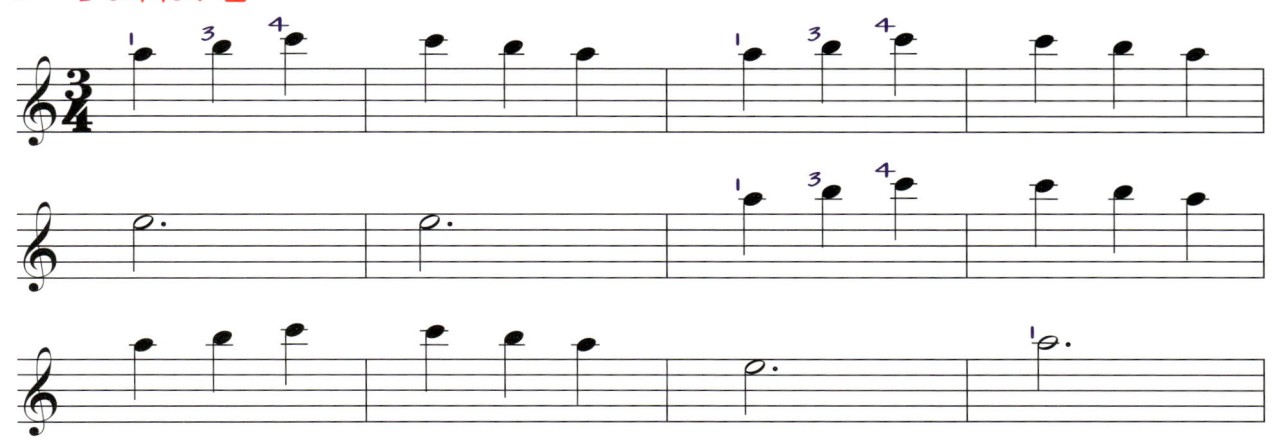

Russhing dance.

The top line of this piece moves from **5th position** to **4th position**. On the **second** line you have to work back down to **1st position**. If your fingers work well they should **dance** all over the **fret board**.

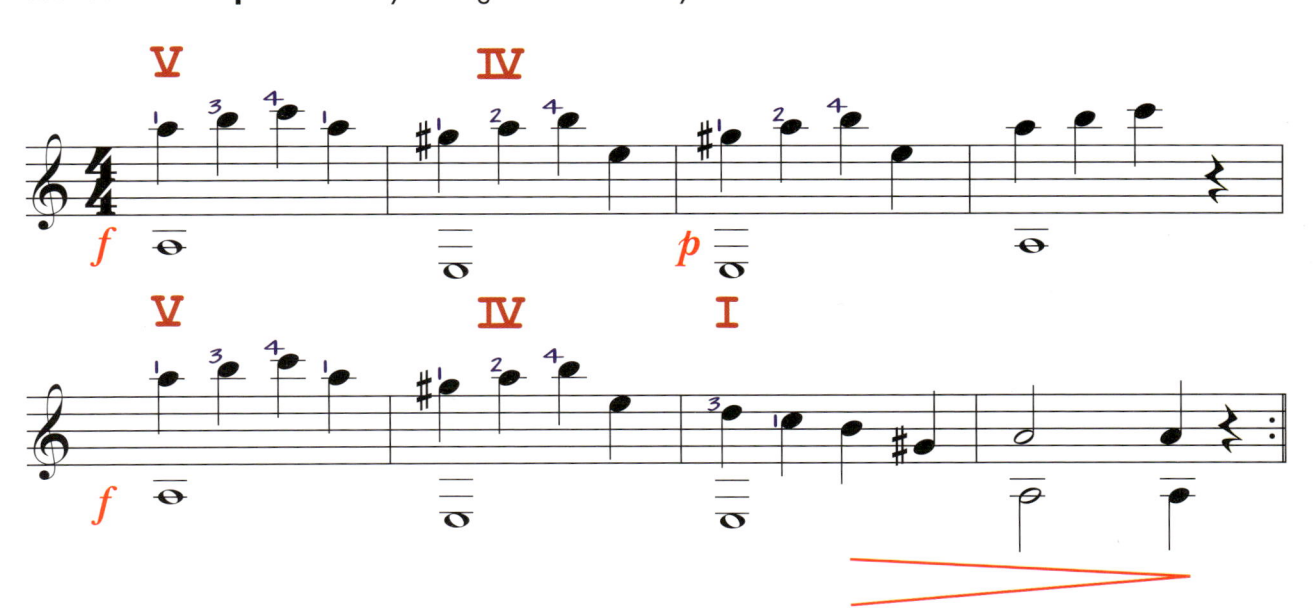

©2005 by Southern Counties Music Publishing. Photocopying is illegal.

Blank staves.

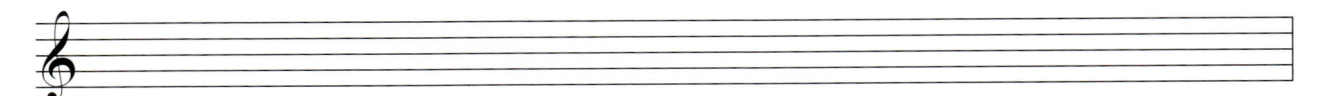

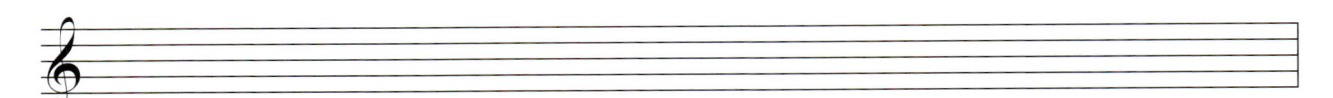

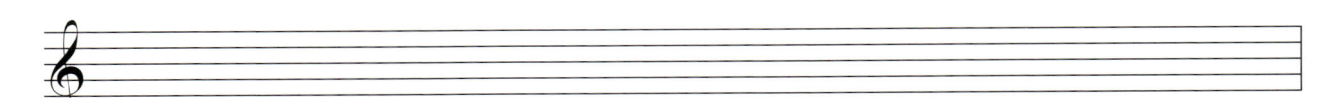

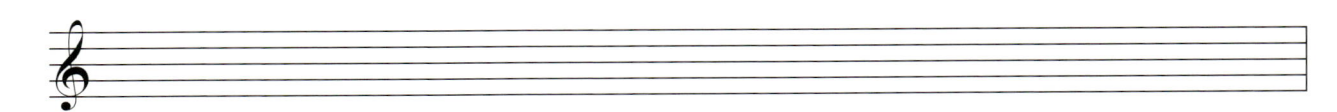

Blank Tab.

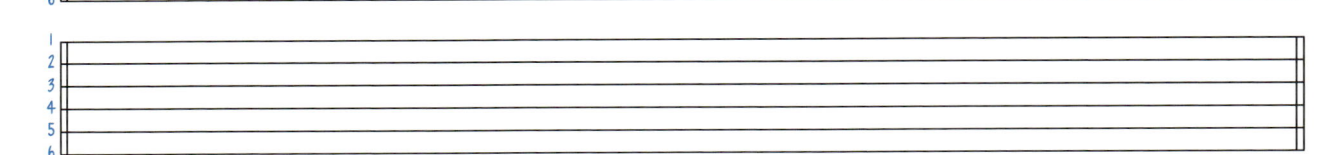

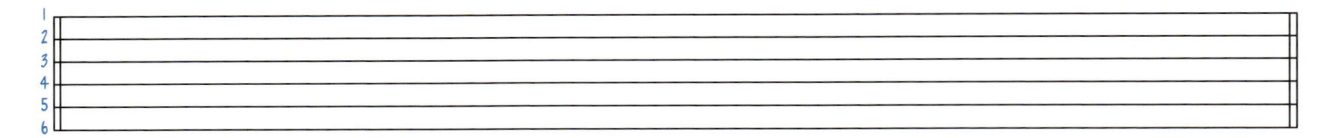

Blank chord blocks.

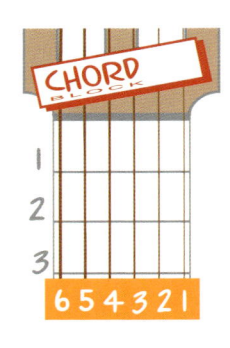

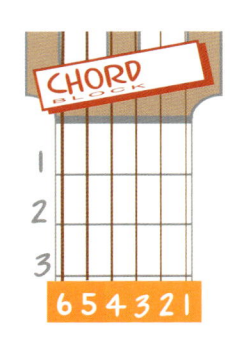

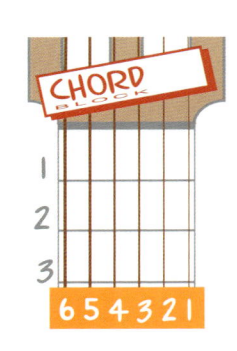

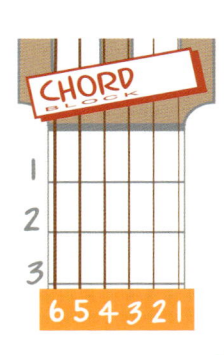

TRAINER CARDS

Carefully cut out along the dotted lines to make a set of 9 Flash cards.

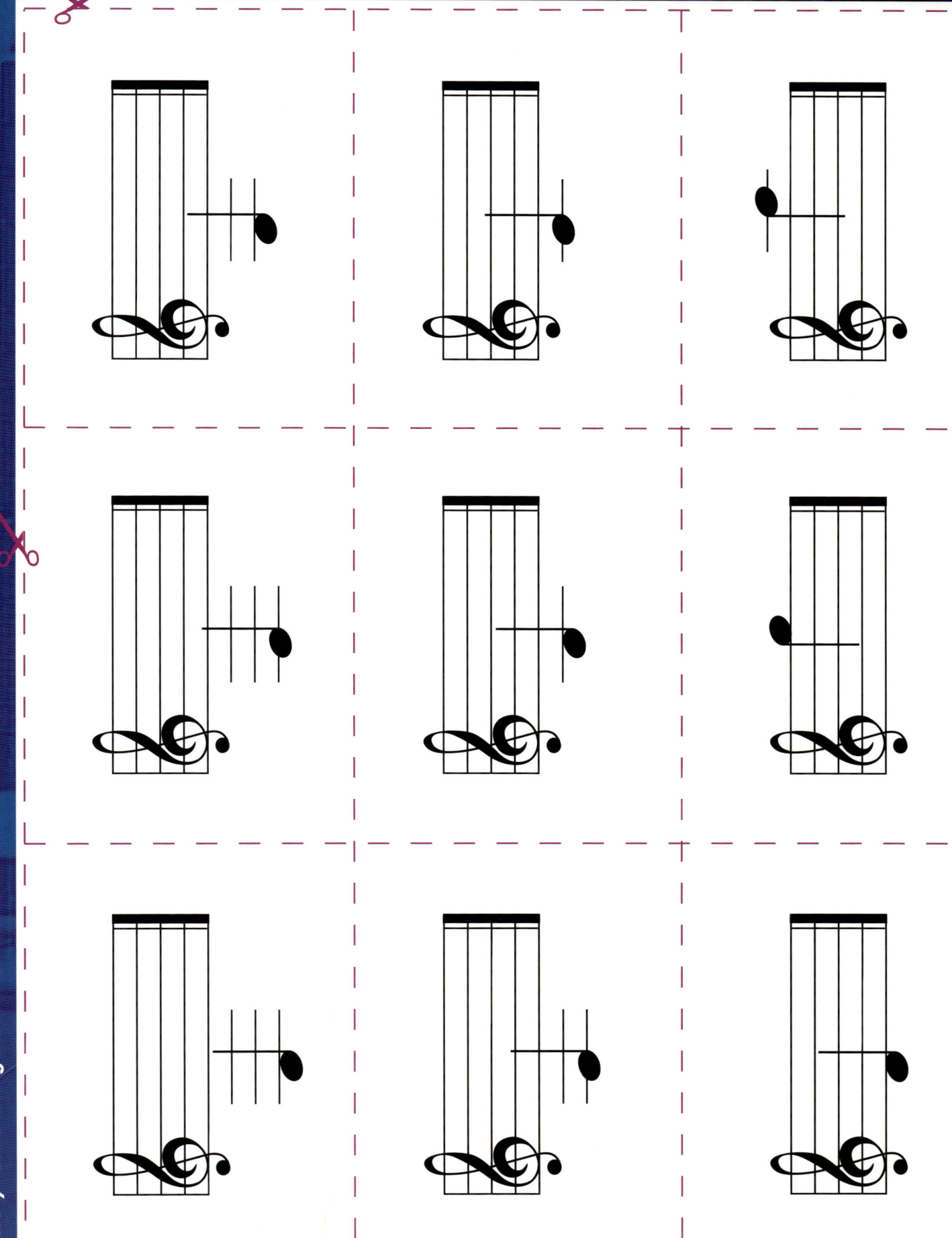

©2005 by Southern Counties Music Publishing. Photocopying is illegal.

23

TRAINER CARDS

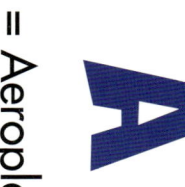

G

C

A
A = Aeroplane

F

B
B = Both ways

G
G = Giant

E

A

D
D = Down below

AWARD CEREMONY

SCAMPS
RAISING THE STANDARDS IN MUSIC EDUCATION

Congratulations.
You have now completed Guitar Trainer Book 3!

©2005 by Southern Counties Music Publishing. Photocopying is illegal.

This is to certify that

_____
STUDENT NAME

has successfully completed

Guitar Trainer Book 3

_____
DATE ACCOMPLISHED

_____
AWARD ACHIEVED

_____
MEDAL PRESENTED

_____
COACH

_____
SIGNATURE OF COACH

SCAMPS

RAISING THE STANDARDS IN MUSIC EDUCATION

©2005 by Southern Counties Music Publishing. Photocopying is illegal.

Guitar Trainer BOOK 3